A FIELD GUIDE TO

FENWAY PARK

AMERICA'S MOST BELOVED BALLPARK

NICHOLE WADSWORTH SCHRAFFT

First published in the United States
of America by:

Twin Lights Publishers, Inc.
8 Hale Street
Rockport, Massachusetts 01966
Telephone: (978) 546-7398
http://www.twinlightspub.com

ISBN: 1-885435-99-1
ISBN: 978-1-885435-99-6

10 9 8 7 6 5 4 3 2 1

Book design by
SYP Design & Production, Inc.
http://www.sypdesign.com

Printed in China

ACKNOWLEDGEMENTS

Growing up on the North Shore, Fenway has always been a part of my quintessential summer and long before I was able to appreciate the game of baseball itself, the ballpark began to exude a certain mystique that has stayed with me throughout my life. When I asked for the opportunity to photograph inside Fenway Park during the 2004 season, I would have never guessed that it would end up being "the season." Four years and two World Series Championships later, I still can't believe that I have been allowed to go along on this unbelievable ride.

I want to thank those within the Red Sox organization who made it possible for me to be there. Thank you to Larry Lucchino for appreciating a teacher/photographer who had a vision and a dream. Thank you to Stacey Lucchino for the endless number of ways she has helped me throughout this process. Thank you to Dr. Charles Steinberg for finding a way for me to earn my keep and thank you to Meg Vaillancourt for all that she has done to help get this book to actual publication. Last but not least, thanks to the players for...well, for everything, after all, they did win the World Series...twice!

We all know how amazing the 2004 and 2007 Red Sox baseball seasons turned out to be and surely none of us will soon forget them, but becoming World Champions isn't the only huge accomplishment the Red Sox should be proud of. While raising millions of dollars, The Red Sox Foundation has become the largest sports foundation in New England and one of the largest in all of Major League Baseball. The ownership's charitable commitment to Boston's community and families throughout New England has been at the forefront of their efforts. They made a pledge to give back to children and they have continued, relentlessly, to do just that.

I am nothing short of honored to say that a portion of the proceeds on the sale of each of these books goes to The Red Sox Foundation. For more information about the children's charitable programs run and supported by the foundation, or to make a donation, please visit www.redsoxfoundation.org.

—Nichole Wadsworth Schrafft

INTRODUCTION

When Larry and I came to Boston, we knew this was a special town. The passion and excitement of the Red Sox was everywhere we went and seemed to be in the eyes of everyone we encountered. From the moment you step into Fenway Park the magical aura surrounds you. You can almost hear and see the memories of generations of children, parents, grandparents and friends who have visited this beloved ballpark. A ballpark located in the heart of Boston and living in the hearts of Bostonians.

We believe baseball fanatics in training, young and old, will enjoy learning the important words and catch phrases of the game. Nichole's photography brings these words to life, capturing the beauty, excitement and the history of both Fenway Park and its exuberant fans with a skilled and creative eye.

Those of us associated with the Red Sox especially appreciate Nichole's generosity in donating a portion of the proceeds from this book to the Red Sox Foundation. The Foundation addresses and lends support to children's health, education, recreation and other difficult urban social issues throughout New England.

We also hope that those who read and enjoy this book will become the newest members of Red Sox Nation.

—Stacey and Larry Lucchino

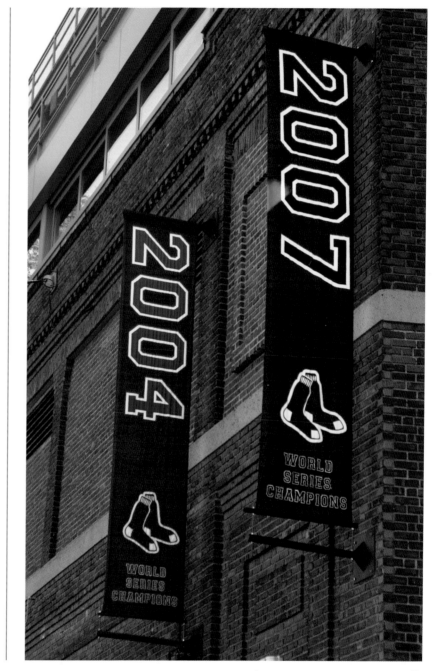

AMERICAN LEAGUE *(proper noun)*

There are two leagues in Major League Baseball. Fourteen teams are a part of the American League. Those teams are from Baltimore, Boston, New York, Tampa Bay, Toronto, Chicago, Cleveland, Detroit, Kansas City, Minnesota, Anaheim, Oakland, Seattle, and Texas. *Can you name the teams from those cities?* I'll get you started; Boston's team is The Boston Red Sox. The pitchers who play in this league do not have a turn to bat during games.

AMERICAN LEAGUE										
P		IN	R	P			IN	R
34	CLE	3		38	DET			
30	TB	0		34	SEA			
33	NYY			49	KC			
45	TEX			40	OAK			
20	CWS				BAL			
57	MIN			34	ANA			

ANNOUNCER *(noun)*

What would a ball game be without the famous voices of the announcers? The announcers sit in the broadcast booth and give play by play action for the radio or television station they work for. Some fans who attend the games in person miss the play by play account so much that they will tune in by means of a portable radio or headset.

ASSIST *(noun)*

When one player fields a ball then throws it to a teammate in order to help him make an out. When a player is successful in helping to throw a runner out he is awarded with an assist in his personal statistics.

One announcer, Jerry Remy, is loved so much at Fenway Park he has a restaurant named after him. It is called REMDAWG'S.

AT BAT *(noun)*

The two teams take turns playing in the field and at bat. When a player is having a turn at bat he is able to continue batting until he has successfully hit the ball, is walked to 1st base, or is called out. While batting, each player must wear a hard batting helmet for protection. The team continues batting until they make three outs. You will learn more about what else can happen during a typical at bat as you read along in this book.

AUTOGRAPH *(noun: an autograph*
Verb: Please autograph my Fenway book.)

Fans young and old love to collect autographs. If you are lucky, players will autograph all sorts of items such as balls, shirts, photos, programs, bats, hats, ticket stubs, and most anything else. Batting practice and pre-game warm-ups are both good times to try to collect autographs, but even then it can be tricky because the players are always really busy. Autographed items can also be purchased in places such as souvenir shops. An item that is autographed and kept in good condition may someday be worth a lot of money, but even if it isn't, it will still bring back great memories of a day at the park.

AVERAGES *(noun)*

People called statisticians keep track of how well players do at bat and in the field. Averages are figured based upon each player's individual performance. Some examples of averages are Batting Average (AVG), Earned Run Average (ERA), and Fielding Average.

B

Bad Call *(noun)*

A decision made by an umpire that is considered unsatisfactory to players, fans, coaches, and/or managers. Although this may not be an official term, it is one that you hear quite often. Sometimes a call will be changed after some discussion has taken place.

Balk *(verb)*

When a pitcher begins to throw a pitch, but stops just prior to releasing the pitch.

(noun) If an umpire calls a balk each player gets to move to the next base.

Ball *(noun)*

A pitch that is thrown outside of a batter's strike zone and is not swung at by the hitter. If a pitch is too high, too low, too far inside, or too far outside, it is called a ball by the umpire. If a pitcher throws four balls, the batter gets to advance to first base *(see walk)*.

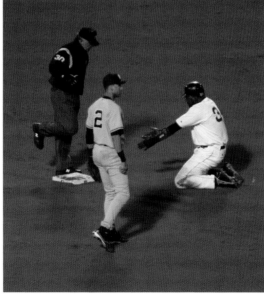

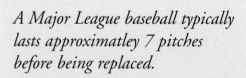

A Major League baseball typically lasts approximatley 7 pitches before being replaced.

BALL BOY AND BALL GIRL
(noun)

Those lucky teenagers who get to sit along the first and third baselines to catch any ball that is not actually in play. If you are lucky and are in the right seat they might even hand the ball to you. Sometimes Wally the Green Monster moonlights as a Ball Boy.

BASE *(noun)*

The white square that is sometimes called a bag represents what we call 1st, 2nd, and 3rd base. Runners hope to move from 1st base, to 2nd base, to 3rd base, and then to home plate. Runners have to touch each base. When a team is playing in the field, players are positioned near each base to try to tag runners on the opposing team out.

BASELINE *(noun)*

The lines drawn from home plate, past 1st and 3rd base, and along the sides of right and left field. These lines define fair from foul territory.

BASE COACH *(noun)*

A coach that stands next to 1st or 3rd base. His job is to help the runner know when to run, when to stay put, or when to steal.

BASES EMPTY (adjective)

When a team is at bat, but no players have made it to base. The players in the field will determine how close or how far away to stand from the actual base depending on whether or not there are runners on base.

BASES LOADED (adjective)

When a team is at bat and they have a runner on 1st, 2nd, and 3rd base. If the home team has the bases loaded the ball park is usually loud and crazy. If the visiting team has the bases loaded it is usually eerily quiet.

BAT (verb)

The act of swinging at the ball. Each player other than the pitcher has a turn to bat.

BAT (noun)

The object used to swing at the ball. Players have their own supply of bats that they use both at home and away. All bats must be made of wood and must meet size, length, and weight regulations. Some players have gotten in trouble for having cork inside of their bats. Corked bats are against the rules in Major League Baseball.

BAT BOY (noun)

The person who gets the appropriate bats ready for the players who are next in the rotation. *(see on-deck)*. He then puts the bats away until that player is ready to bat again.

BATTER'S BOX (noun)

An area around home plate outlined in chalk that indicates where the batter needs to stand. He must request a time-out if he needs to step outside of that box once the pitcher has prepared to pitch.

BATTERY *(noun)*

Pitcher + Catcher = Battery

The pitcher and the catcher need to work very closely together. The pitcher must be able to read the catcher's signals to know what type of pitch to throw. The catcher must have spent a good deal of time practicing with a pitcher so that he can catch his pitches well.

BATTING AVERAGE (AVG) *(noun)*

In the A section you learned about some different types of averages. A player's batting average can be figured out by counting the number of base hits he has had and then dividing that number by his total times at bat. So:

base hits ÷ turns at bat = AVG

If a player has hit 10 different base hits and has had 30 turns at bat it would look like this:

$$10 \div 30 = .333$$

Sometimes the scoreboard will show how a certain batter has done against the pitcher he is currently facing.

Can you show how to figure out the AVG for a player who has batted 15 times and has had five hits?

BATTING ORDER *(noun)*

The order in which the players take turns at bat. Nine players rotate turns at bat and stay in the same predetermined order for the entire game. A substitution can be made where a new player will take over someone else's position in the batting order.

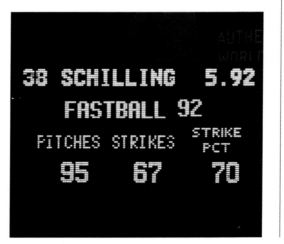

BATTING PRACTICE *(noun)*

A designated time before a game when the teams get to practice batting. In Fenway Park a lot of balls end up soaring over the famous Green Monster and right out of the park. If you are able to stand in the new Green Monster seats you might even catch a ball.

BEAN *(verb)*

When a pitcher hits the batter with a pitch.

BEANBALL *(noun)*

A pitch that is thrown with the intention of hitting the batter. This is obviously frowned upon and often times results in an argument between teams.

BEHIND *(preposition)*

In the C section you will learn about the *count*. If a pitcher has thrown more balls than strikes he is considered to be behind the batter. If the batter has received more strikes than balls, he is considered to be

behind the pitcher. Obviously neither of the players wants to be behind in the *count*.

BLEACHERS *(noun)*

The seats in Fenway Park that are located behind centerfield. The bleacher seats are the least expensive seats in the park and they usually become the loudest. The fans who sit there are sometimes called Bleacher Creatures. You will often see beach balls being tossed around in the bleachers. If you sit there plan on getting some sun. A section was closed because the activity of the fans was found to be distracting to the players at bat. Sometimes green shirts will be handed out to fans during day games so that they blend in with the seats and the walls and are less visually distracting.

BELIEVE *(verb)*

(I Believe, We Believe)

The act of accepting something as truth or reality. Red Sox fans have believed in their team season after season. 2004 proved to be the year that fans could finally say, "We Believed" as their beliefs turned into the first Red Sox World Series Championship in 86 years. Fans kept the faith and were rewarded with another Championship only 3 short years later! Now that's something to "Believe" in!

BOBBLE (verb)

To fumble a ball that is in play.

BULLPEN (noun)

An area where relief pitchers and catchers sit during games. The bullpen provides them with the space they need to practice and warm-up in case they are needed during the game. A telephone is connected between the dugout and the bullpen so that a call can be made to tell players when to begin preparing.

Sometimes almost all of the relief pitchers are used during a game and occasionally none of them are. *(see Complete Game)*. Both the home team and the visiting team have a bullpen in each ballpark.

BUNT (verb)

When the batter intentionally hits the ball a very short distance by holding the bat almost horizontally and turning his body into the pitch. A player bunts so that one or more of the infielders will have to run in towards home plate to get the ball. This maneuver helps a base runner advance to the next base.

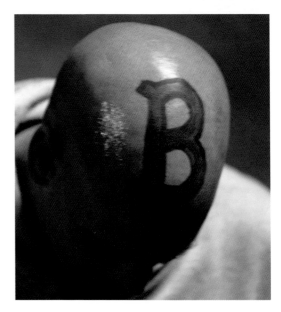

C

CALLED GAME (noun)

The term used to describe a game that an umpire has ended before the official 9th inning ending.

CANNON (noun)

The name for the arm of a player who has the ability to throw the ball very long distances.

CANVAS ALLEY (proper noun)

The place where the grounds crew sits during the game. They wait to rake the base path or cover the field in case of rain. Canvas Alley is located about half way down the right field baseline. The canvas tarp that is used to cover the field during rain used to be kept here.

Fenway's playing surface was redone in 2004 which will now allow for better drainage and shorter rain delays.

CATCHER (noun)

The player who stands behind the batter and home plate to catch the pitcher's throws. He communicates with the pitcher to help determine what pitches to throw by using predetermined signs. The catcher must stay within the *catcher's box* until the ball leaves the pitcher's hand.

CENTERFIELD (noun)

The middle of the outfield behind 2nd base. Inside Fenway Park a homerun hit to centerfield can be 420 feet.

CEREMONIAL FIRST PITCH (noun)

During pre-game activities someone is given the honor of throwing a pitch to signify the beginning of the game. After the pitch you will hear the famous words "Play Ball!"

CHECK SWING (noun)

An incomplete swing. Sometimes a batter will begin to swing at a pitch and decide not to and stop the swing. If the umpire concludes that the batter was swinging at the ball then a strike will be called.

CITGO SIGN (noun)

A famous Fenway Park Landmark. This huge neon sign is located high above Kenmore Square and can be seen from many locations throughout the city of Boston.

CLEAN-UP HITTER (noun)

The name given to the player who bats fourth in the batting order. If the first three batters have made it to base this player has the opportunity to hit a grand slam and clear (clean) the bases.

CLOSER (noun)

The pitcher who is favored to get the last few outs of the game. A closer is usually used to hold a lead in the last inning or two.

CLUBHOUSE (noun)

A place for team members, staff, and media only. The clubhouse is where the locker rooms are located and where teams hold their private meetings. Just as students decorate their lockers at school, baseball players will often hang photos and personal items in their lockers.

COACH (noun)

As we all know, behind every good team there are great coaches. The Red Sox have a 1st base coach, a 3rd base coach, a pitching coach, a batting coach, and a bench coach.

COMPLETE GAME (noun)

When the starting pitcher pitches an entire game.

CONCOURSE (noun)

The area inside of the ballpark located underneath and behind all of the seats. This is where fans go to buy refreshments and sometimes to get out of bad weather. Fenway Park added a new concourse in 2004 that is full of comfortable tables and a variety of food choices.

CONIGLIARO'S CORNER (noun)

Conigliaro's Corner was added before the 2007 season and created 200 bleacher seats on the Right Field Roof. They are named after Tony Conigliaro, a hometown favorite player, and are priced at $25 to pay tribute to the number he wore.

COUNT (noun)

During an at bat the pitches thrown are labeled as balls or strikes. The count indicates how many of each has been thrown. The umpire usually holds up fingers to remind the players of what the current count is. Fans can also look at the scoreboard to see where the batter stands in the count.

CROWDING THE PLATE (verb)

Okay, so this picture doesn't actually show what it means to crowd the plate, but I bet it is what you imagined when you heard the term! When a batter stands really close to home plate he is said to be crowding the plate. Batters do this if he thinks the pitcher is going to throw a pitch to the outside of the plate.

CUT-OFF MAN (noun)

A player who catches a ball, usually thrown by an outfielder, and then throws it along to yet another player to get a runner out. The distance between the extreme outfield and home plate is very far. For more accuracy an infielder will often catch the ball midway and then throw to a base.

CYCLE (noun)

When a batter hits a single, a double, a triple, and a homerun during the same game. The last Red Sox player to hit for the cycle was John Valentin in 1996. Bobby Doerr is the only Red Sox player to hit for the cycle twice.

DEFENSE *(noun)*

The team that is currently playing in the field.

DESIGNATED HITTER (DH) *(noun)*

The Designated Hitter bats for the pitcher and does not play in the field. Only the American League uses the DH. It is generally assumed that the DH is a valuable batter with a good AVG.

DIMCOCK CENTER *(noun)*

A non-profit institution in Roxbury that provides health care, social services, and educational programs to more than 40,000 families in Boston's most disadvantaged neighborhoods. As one of the Red Sox Foundations' "4 cornerstone programs," the Dimock Community Health Center and the team charity have partnered with Microsoft and CityYear to support after school programs for inner city children and teens.

DINGER *(noun)*

A commonly used expression for homerun. As in, "He hit a real dinger!" In this photo the umpire is pointing and moving his hand in a circular motion to indicate that the hit was indeed a homerun…or dinger.

DISABLED LIST *(noun)*

A list of players who are not able to play due to injury. This list is often times referred to as the DL.

DIVISIONS *(noun)*

The *American League* and the *National League* each have three regional divisions: the Eastern Division, the Central Division, and the Western Division. All three divisions within a league play against each other throughout the season.

DONUT *(noun)*

A heavy weight that is slid onto the bat while a batter is practicing.

DOUBLE *(noun)*

When a batter hits the ball and makes it to second base safely he is credited with a double.

DOUBLE HEADER *(noun)*

When two teams play each other twice in the same day. The second game can either immediately follow the first or it can be played that night for what is called a *Day/Night Double Header*.

DOUBLE PLAY *(noun)*

When two outs are made during the same play. In order to create a double play there must already be at least one runner on base. When a runner is on base the fielders reflexively know where to throw the ball to turn the double play for two quick outs.

DUGOUT *(noun)*

The place where teams sit during the game. Only team members, coaches, staff, and managers are allowed to sit in the dugout during game time. Each ballpark has a home team and visiting team dugout. The dugouts have immediate access to the clubhouse.

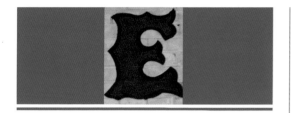

EARNED RUN (noun)

When a pitcher is responsible for a run scored by the opposing team that was not the result of a fielder's error.

EARNED RUN AVERAGE (ERA) (noun)

Another one of the averages mentioned earlier. This average is only applicable to a pitcher. A pitcher's ERA is calculated by taking the number of Earned Runs, multiplying that by nine, and then dividing that product by how many innings he has pitched in all. So:

(Earned Runs x 9) ÷ number of innings pitched = ERA

Let's say a pitcher has been responsible for opposing teams scoring 49 runs.

49 x 9 = 441

He has pitched a total of 121 innings.

441 ÷ 121 = 3.64.

A pitcher wants as low of an ERA as possible.

EQUIPMENT (noun)

All of the gear and items that are essential to the players being able to play the game properly. Players have their own bats, batting helmets, batting gloves, baseball gloves, and uniforms plus much, much more. Catcher's have more equipment than other team members so they remain safe while catching balls that are sometimes thrown at close to 100 mph. An equipment manager is responsible for making sure that everything is packed for away games.

ERROR (noun)

When a defensive player fails to catch a ball that could have been fielded and it results in a runner getting on base or advancing to another base. Errors are recorded on the scoreboard and are also part of each player's statistics.

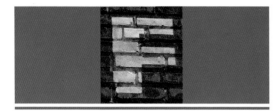

FAIR *(adjective, as in* fair ball *or* fair territory*)*

Within or touching the lines/boundaries that designate the playing field. A *fair ball* is one that is batted within what is regarded as *fair territory*. Balls hit towards second base or centerfield are obviously fair, but when balls are hit to far right or far left field it can be hard to judge whether they will land in or out of fair territory. Fair territory is marked with lines that begin at the batter's box and extend beyond both 1st and 3rd base. If a batted ball lands on those lines the ball is still considered fair.

FAN *(verb)*

To swing at a pitch and miss. As with an actual fan, a breeze is created by the strong swinging of the bat. A strike is called.

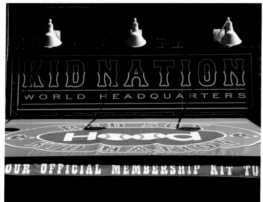

FAN *(noun)*

One who enjoys, follows, roots for, supports, and encourages a player or team. While doing so, a fan becomes vulnerable to heartbreak and pain or makes it possible to share in triumph and victory.

FANATIC (noun)

A fan who has passionate enthusiasm and profound devotion to the team.

FARM TEAM (noun)

A minor league baseball team that is affiliated with a major league baseball team. The farm teams are categorized by A (single A), AA (double A), or AAA (triple A) ratings with AAA being closest to the major leagues. The Boston Red Sox have several farm teams: The Pawtucket Red Sox in Rhode Island, the Portland Sea Dogs in Maine, the Wilmington Blue Rocks in Delaware, the Capital City Bombers in South Carolina, and the Lowell Spinners in Massachusetts.

FENWAY PARK (proper noun)

Home to the Boston Red Sox and located in Boston, Massachusetts. Fenway Park got its name by then owner, John I. Taylor, who decided to build the new ballpark in the area of Boston known as the Fens. The very first Opening Day at Fenway was on April 20th, 1912. Luck was not on the ballpark's side as it suffered two fires within eight years of each other. The second of the two fires damaged a huge portion of the park, but it still opened successfully for opening day of the 1934 season. Today Fenway Park looks very different than it did in 1912, but it still remains one of the oldest and most historic ballparks in baseball.

FIELD *(noun)*

The grass playing surface. The field's dimensions are 302 feet along the right field line, 420 feet in deep centerfield, and 310 feet along the left field line.

FIELDING AVERAGE *(noun)*

A statistic used to evaluate a fielders performance. A fielding average is calculated by using the number of outs a fielder has directly made (put outs), how many assists he has had, and how many errors he has committed.

(Put outs + *assists*) ÷ (*put outs* + *assists* + *errors*) = *fielding average*

FIRST BASE *(noun)*

Where a batter runs first upon hitting a ball. First base is marked with a square white bag and is located 90 feet from home plate, 90 feet from 2nd base, and 127' 3 3/8" from 3rd base.

FIRST BASE DECK *(noun)*

A new First Base Deck was added in 2006 to create more standing room and extra concession stands behind the grandstands.

FIRST BASEMAN *(noun)*

The defensive player manning 1st base. If there is not a runner on 1st base, the first baseman usually stands behind the actual base to allow him to better field balls hit beyond the immediate infield. If a runner is on 1st base, he will stand directly at 1st base to prevent stolen bases and assist in a double play if another ball is hit. A first baseman must tag the actual base or the runner to get an out.

FISK'S POLE *(proper noun)*

The Left Field foul pole named after Carlton Fisk as a tribute to his 12th inning homerun against the Cincinnati Reds that resulted in winning Game 6 of the 1975 World Series. The Red Sox ultimately lost the Series during Game 7.

FLY BALL *(noun)*

A ball hit really high into the outfield so that the fielder can get underneath it and catch it without difficulty.

FORCED PLAY *(noun)*

When a runner must advance to the next base because another runner is advancing behind him. If there is a forced play the defensive player need only tag the base before the runner gets there and then throw the ball to another player to assist in a double or even triple play.

FOUL *(adjective)*

Outside of fair territory. A foul ball is one that is hit into foul territory. If a ball is hit outside of the base lines (foul lines), and is caught by a defensive player it's an out. It is not uncommon to see players crashing into the crowd or dugouts in an attempt to catch a ball hit into foul territory.

FOUL TIP *(noun)*

A ball that is tipped off of a player's bat directly into the glove of the catcher. When this ball is caught it is counted as a strike.

FULL COUNT *(noun)*

When the pitch count for a particular at bat has reached 3 balls and 2 strikes. A full count suggests that the next pitch will end the at bat whether it be a ball or a strike. If a foul ball is hit with two strikes, however, the at bat continues.

.406 CLUB *(proper noun)*

The .406 Club was named in honor of Ted Williams .406 AVG during the 1941 baseball season. Prior to the 2006 Season the Red Sox removed the glass that had separated the .406 Club from the excitement and energy of Fenway Park and in doing so created the "EMC Club" and the "State Street Pavilion." The changes added 1,300 seats, lots of standing room and additional concession stands.

GOLD GLOVE (noun)

An award created in 1957 by the Rawlings baseball glove manufacturer that is given to players from each position who have excelled during the season. In 2007 Kevin Youkilis was awarded the Gold Glove for his outstanding season as a first baseman. In 2005, Red Sox catcher, Jason Varitek was a Gold Glove recipient.

GRAND SLAM (noun)

A homerun that is hit when the bases are already loaded. A Grand Slam scores 4 runs.

GRANDSTAND (noun)

A section of seats within the ballpark. Grandstand seats are in the back half of the lower level. They are behind the field boxes and the loge seats and they extend to the very top of the lower level.

GREEN LIGHT (noun)

Permission given to the runner to decide when he thinks it is safe to steal. It also gives the batter permission to swing on the next pitch.

J.D. Drew hit a first-inning Grand Slam during Game 6 of the American League Championship against the Cleveland Indians in 2007 that helped the Sox come back from a 3 games to 1 deficit and go on to and eventually win Game 7.

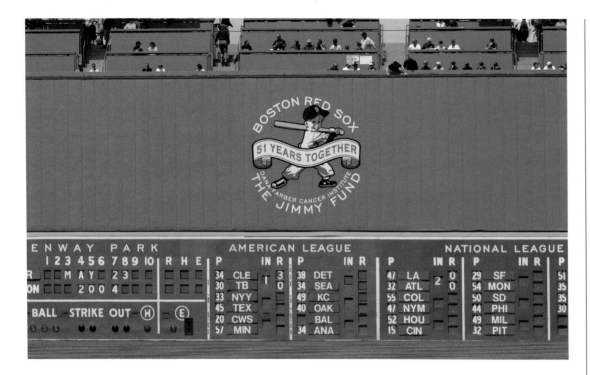

GROUNDS CREW (noun)

The people responsible for the care and upkeep of the field. The grounds crew works year round and must be available immediately in the case of rain to help protect the field. Keeping the field looking perfect is an awesome responsibility that requires the hard work of many. The field is mowed every single day of the baseball season and will often have patterns cut into the grass.

GREEN MONSTER (proper noun)

The left field wall inside of Fenway Park. The Green Monster is 37 feet high and is a defining feature of the ballpark. Homeruns hit over the Green Monster are known for bouncing off of cars parked on the city streets outside of the park. In 2004 additional seats, called the Monster Seats, were added on top of the wall.

GROUND BALL (noun)

A ball that bounces in the infield after being hit.

GROUND RULES (noun)

Rules that have been predetermined for different situations that may happen throughout a ball game in a specific ball park. One of the most common is a Ground Rule Double. If a ball is hit into the outfield, bounces, and then lands in the stands, the runner is only allowed to advance to second base as opposed to running all the way home for a homerun.

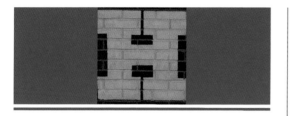

HIGH AND INSIDE *(adjective)*

Describes a pitch that has been thrown very close to a batter's face. This pitch is sometimes called *Chin Music*. A pitcher may throw this pitch if he believes the batter is *crowding the plate*.

HIT *(verb)*

The act of hitting a ball and arriving safely on base.

(noun)

A batter will not be credited with a hit if a fielder's error made it possible for him to make it on base.

HOMERUN *(noun)*

When the batter hits a pitch and makes it all the way around the bases, returning safely to home plate.

In 2004 the Red Sox became the only team to ever come back from a 0-3 deficit to go to win a seven game series. That history-making feat led to their American League Championship and ultimately to a World Series Championship. In 2007 the Red Sox came back from a 3-1 deficit during the ALCS to win it all again!

IN PLAY *(adjective)*

To currently be in the midst of a play. If a ball is in play it is a live ball.

IN THE DIRT *(adjective)*

A pitch that falls short of the catcher. Occasionally a pitch will be thrown too low and will bounce in the dirt in front of the catcher's glove. This is obviously a horrible pitch and not one that a pitcher throws intentionally.

IN THE PARK HOMERUN *(noun)*

A homerun that is made when the ball is hit inside the playing field. Most home-runs happen when the ball is hit into the stands or even out of the park. In that case, a runner can take his time rounding the bases. When a runner is trying to make it home with a ball still in play he really has to hustle!

INFIELD (noun)

The section of the field that lies within home plate, 1st base, 2nd base, and 3rd base.

INNING (noun)

A period of time during which both teams have a turn to bat and to play in the field. Once both teams have made three outs that particular inning is over. When the first team is at bat it is called the top of the inning. Once their turn is over and the second team is at bat it is called the bottom of the inning. The visiting team always bats in the top of the inning. A regulation game is 9 innings long, but can be shorter if it is called because of rain, suspended by the umpires, or if the home team is winning at the end of the top of the 9th inning. There is no reason for them to bat again if they already have the lead. A game can also be much longer than 9 innings if the score remains tied.

INTENTIONAL WALK (noun)

When a pitcher throws four balls to the batter on purpose. When a pitcher plans on intentionally walking a batter the catcher will stand off to the side and catch the balls outside of the batter's strike zone. An intentional walk may be executed to prevent a really strong batter from hitting in runs or to create a forced play.

INTERFERENCE (noun)

When a spectator gets in the way of a player and prevents him from making a play. Interference can also happen between teams and would then be called Offensive Interference or Defensive Interference depending on which team did the interfering. Sometimes umpires can even be guilty of interference.

THE JIMMY FUND

(proper noun)

The Jimmy Fund supports the fight against cancer in children and adults at The Dana-Farber Cancer Institute in Boston. Over 50 years ago the Red Sox adopted the Jimmy Fund as its official charity and have continued to support the cause in truly astounding ways.

K *(noun)*

A strikeout. A "K" is given when the batter strikes out while swinging. A backwards or upside down "K" is given when the batter strikes out looking and doesn't swing.

K-MEN *(proper noun)*

A group of 8 fans (and sometimes their friends) who, during certain games, place large letter K signs high above the outfield to record strikeouts made by Red Sox pitchers. The K-men typically dress in red and even paint their faces. They say that the most Ks they have hung up is 17.

LADDER (noun)

A structure used for climbing up and down heights. If a ball hits the ladder on the Green Monster at Fenway Park it is still in play.

LEAD (noun)

The higher score. The team that is winning has the lead.

The score is 6 to 3 and the Red Sox have the lead.

(verb)

1. To be ahead in the score. The Red Sox are leading.

2. When a runner steps off of his base to begin advancing towards the next base. Sometimes pitchers will allow runners to take a lead and other times they will try to throw them out. Runners must tag the base in between each pitch.

LEFT FIELD (noun)

The part of the outfield behind 3rd base. In Fenway Park the Left Field is in front of the Green Monster. It is 310 feet along the Left Field Line and 379 feet in deep left field.

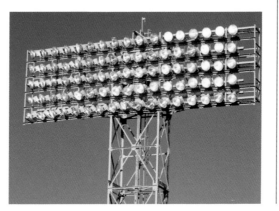

LIGHTS (noun)

Seven separate light towers make night games look like daytime with their huge, round light bulbs. In all there are 544 bulbs. Trust me, I counted them over and over again to be sure.

Show how *bright* you can be!

If light tower #1 has 60 bulbs

#2 has 95 bulbs

#3 has 52 bulbs

#4 has 78 bulbs

#5 has 85 bulbs

and #6 has 114 bulbs

How many bulbs are in light tower #7?

LINE DRIVE *(noun)*

A ball that is hit by the batter, but does not travel very far off the ground. If they are hit very hard, line drives can be dangerous to the pitcher or other infield players.

LINE-UP *(noun)*

A list of players, the order they will be batting in, and the positions they will be playing while in the field. Both teams must complete this list and give it to the officials before the game begins. Changes may not be made unless a substitution is made and another player comes in to replace an existing player. There are ten players in a line-up: the pitcher, catcher, 1st baseman, 2nd baseman, 3rd baseman, shortstop, right fielder, center fielder, left fielder, and the designated hitter.

LOOKING *(verb)*

When a batter is struck out without swinging at the pitch, he is caught looking. The batter is looking without swinging because he believes the pitch is going to be out of his strike zone and called a *ball*.

M

MAGIC NUMBERS (noun)

The number of games that a team needs to win in order to make the play-offs. To figure out a team's magic numbers:

Take the number of games left to be played, add one, and then subtract the number of games that they are ahead of the team closest to them in the standings.

If a team had 30 games left and they were four games ahead of the next team their Magic Number would be 27.

30 (games left) + 1 = 31
31-4 (games ahead) = 27

MANAGER (noun)

The person who is in charge of the team's activity. The manager may consult with the different coaches and together they decide on the starting line-up, substitutions, pitching changes, and plays.

MEATBALL (noun)

A pitch that is fairly easy to hit. A meatball is usually thrown kind of slow and right over the middle of the plate. How far do you think a batter could hit a real meatball? I wouldn't want to have to catch it!

MOUND (noun)

The round area where the pitcher stands to deliver pitches. Many rules apply to the mound and to what the pitcher is allowed, or not allowed, to do while on the mound. A rubber pitcher's plate indicates where on the mound the pitcher should stand. The distance between the pitcher's plate and home plate must be 60 feet and 6 inches, the mound must be 10 inches higher than home plate, and it must be 18 feet in diameter.

MVP (noun)

The abbreviation for *Most Valuable Player*. An MVP is selected at the end of each game. MVPs are also chosen for play-off series.

Just three short years after Manny Ramirez was named the 2004 World Series MVP, Red Sox 3rd Baseman, Mike Lowell, was given the same honor thanks to his great performance during the 2007 World Series.

NATIONAL ANTHEM *(noun)*

Francis Scott Key wrote the *Star Spangled Banner* in 1814 while detained on a British Ship within view of Fort McHenry. In 1931 Congress voted it our national anthem. It is now proudly played or sung before all professional sporting events. It is customary for fans and players to stand and remove their caps as a sign of respect.

NATIONAL LEAGUE *(proper noun)*

The collective name for sixteen teams who play each other for a league championship. Can you connect each team to their home?

Home	Team Name
Atlanta	Cardinals
Philadelphia	Nationals
Florida	Diamond Backs
New York	Brewers
Wash. D.C.	Dodgers
St. Louis	Braves
Houston	Giants
Chicago	Rockies
Cincinnati	Marlins
Pittsburgh	Padres
Milwaukee	Mets
Los Angeles	Cubs
San Francisco	Reds
San Diego	Phillies
Colorado	Astros
Arizona	Pirates

Do you know which National League team changed hometowns after the 2004 baseball season?

Answer: The Montreal Expos, who are now the Washington Nationals

NIGHT GAME *(noun)*

A game played in the evening under the lights.

NO HITTER *(noun)*

A credit given to a pitcher who does not allow any batter to earn a hit during the course of a game.

NUMBER ONE *(noun)*

To be in first place. As in, "We're Number One!" Red Sox fans have been able to claim this spot in the years 1903, 1912, 1915, 1916, 1918, 2004, and 2007.

OFFENSE (noun)

When a team is at bat they are the offense. When a team is playing in the field they are playing defense.

ON-BASE PERCENTAGE (OBP) (noun)

A statistic given to batters. To figure out a batter's OBP you need to factor in a lot of information. The math would look like this:

(Total number of hits +
Bases on Balls + Hit by Pitch)

÷

(At Bats + Bases on Balls +
Hit by Pitch + Sacrifice Flies)

ON DECK CIRCLE (noun)

The place where the batter who is up next stands to warm up.

OPS (noun)

Statistic that combines a players On Base Percentage and Slugging Percentage by simply adding them together.

OUTFIELD (noun)

The large area of field beyond the infield. The outfield is divided between left, right, and center field and is covered by three individual *outfielders*.

OUT (noun)

The term when a batter or runner is removed from play by a defensive player. A batter can strike out while at bat or become out as a player fields the ball.

(adjective)

The status of a player. As in, "He is out."

PASSED BALL *(noun)*

When the catcher fails to catch a pitch and a runner is able to advance.

PENNANT *(noun)*

The name of the American League or National League Championship title. Also a banner or flag given to the championship winners. At Fenway Park pennants hang proudly on Yawkey Way and in the Right Field concourse. American League Championships pennants are blue and World Series Champion pennants are red.

PHOTOGRAPHERS' PIT *(noun)*

An area reserved for photographers to sit and take pictures of the game.

PERFECT GAME *(noun)*

When a pitcher does not allow a single runner to get on base.

PESKY POLE *(proper noun)*

The yellow right field foul pole, named after Johnny Pesky. Pesky only hit 6 homeruns at Fenway, but sources say they all went near that foul pole. One of his homeruns, hit in 1950, ended up winning the game for the Red Sox.

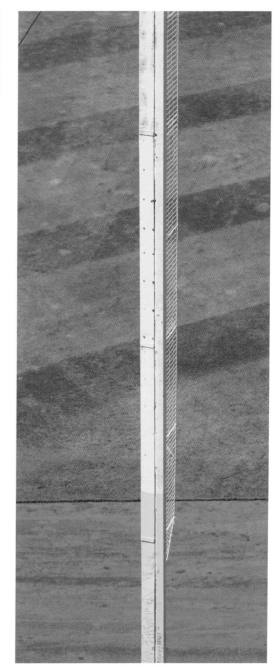

PICKED OFF *(verb)*

When a base runner is thrown or tagged out while trying to get a head start to the next base. When there are runners on base the pitcher needs to be aware of how much of a lead they are taking. If he thinks they are going to steal he will attempt to pick them off.

PICKLE *(noun)*

When a base runner gets caught between two defensive players. This can also be called a run down.

PINCH HITTER *(noun)*

A player who is substituted to bat for another player.

PINCH RUNNER *(noun)*

A player who comes in to run for a player who is currently on base.

PITCHER (noun)

The player responsible for throwing the ball to the batter. Each team has many pitchers. Some pitchers rotate in the starting position while other pitchers are typically used later in the game as relief pitchers or closers. Pitchers who specialize in closing a game are better known for being able to throw for just one or two innings before tiring their arm. Some pitchers are better for throwing to right-handed batters,  some to left-handed batters, and some can throw equally as well to both. Pitchers are credited with either a Win, Loss, or No Decision based on how many innings they pitched and what the score was when they exited the game.

PITCHES (noun)

The many different ways to deliver the ball to the batter. There are many different types of pitches including: fastballs, curveballs, knuckleballs, sliders, sinkers, change-ups, and breaking balls.

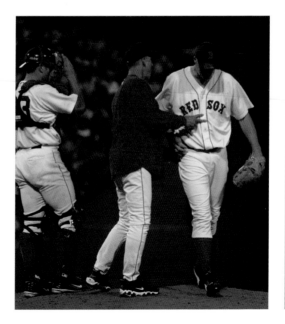

PITCHING ROTATION (noun)

The order in which starting pitchers take turns leading off on the mound. It is typical for starting pitchers to start every 5th game.

POINT (*verb*)

I don't know what it means or how it started, but you sure do see a lot of it happening in and around Fenway Park!

There's the one-handed point, the double point, the thumbs up point, and even the point with a little hip action.

POP-UP FLY (noun)

A ball hit high in the infield and usually caught by an infielder. They don't travel into the outfield.

POST SEASON (noun)

The games played after the regular season has ended to determine which two teams make it to the World Series. The winners of the Eastern Division, Central Division, Western Division, and one wildcard team make it to the play-offs for both the National League and the American League (so eight teams in all). Each League champion then advances to the World Series to play each other.

PRESS BOX (noun)

The place where sports writers sit to watch the game, write articles, and record statistics. The Press Box at Fenway Park is in the highest part of the glassed-in area behind home plate. An updated and improved press box was added for opening day in 2007.

QUALITY START (noun)

When a pitcher pitches at least six innings before leaving the game and allows only three or fewer Earned Runs.

QUIZ (noun)

Attendance is kept at each game by scanning all of the tickets as fans enter the ballpark. Staff, employees, media, security, etc. must enter separately so that an accurate count can also be taken as the turnstiles spin to let fans enter. During the eighth inning spectators can take a guess at what the game's attendance is during the Attendance Quiz. As of 2007, Fenway can hold about 38,808 and is expected to soon reach 39,928. There were 93 home games in 2007 including the World Series.

RAIN DELAY *(noun)*

A team can decide to delay the beginning of a game or even cancel and postpone a game before it begins due to bad weather. Once the game has started, only the officials can decide to stop the game. When it rains at Fenway Park the grounds crew covers the field with a canvas tarp to protect it from damage and flooding.

RBI LEAGUE *(noun)*

Recreational programs supported by the Red Sox Foundation that teach the lessons of life, leadership, and teamwork through sport. The Red Sox Rookie League introduces baseball to 5-12 year old children. RBI stands for Reviving Baseball in Inner Cities and teaches baseball skills to boys and girls between the ages of 13-18 from economically disadvantaged areas. The program also promotes positive conflict resolution, seeks to raise self-esteem, and instills good values within participants.

RED SOX *(proper noun)*

In the year 1901 the then Boston Americans joined the American League. They were briefly called other names like The Puritans and The Pilgrims, but in 1907 they were renamed The Boston Red Sox. Although the name suggests that the Sox belong to Boston, fans from all of the New England states actually support and root for the team.

RED SOX FOUNDATION

(proper noun)

The part of the Red Sox organization that oversees charitable donations. Since their founding in 2002, the foundation's mission is to improve the health, educational, and recreational opportunities for children in New England through non-profit contributions to the four cornerstones of the foundation including the Jimmy Fund, the Dimock Center, the RBI League, and the Red Sox Scholars.

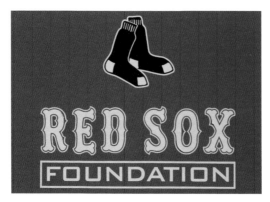

RED SOX NATION *(proper noun)*

A Red Sox Fan Club that you can join to become an official member. Although Red Sox Nation is in fact a real club, many people use the saying "Red Sox Nation" to refer to the fans that live all over this country and not just in the New England area. Although the team's home is obviously in Boston, Red Sox fans can be found in every state of the union and around the world.

RED SOX SCHOLARS *(proper noun)*

The 25 academically-talented yet economically-disadvantaged Boston 5th graders selected each year by the Red Sox Foundation as Red Sox Scholars. They receive mentoring and college scholarship funds. The scholarships are dependant on good grades and citizenship. One of the 4 cornerstones of the Red Sox Foundation, the program also works with Beth Israel Medical Center to introduce 6th grade scholars to various health professions.

RELIEF PITCHERS *(noun)*

The pitchers who stay in the bullpen and prepare to enter the game when the starting pitcher or other relievers are pulled from the game.

RETIRED NUMBERS *(noun)*

The numbers that current players are not allowed to wear on their jerseys because they have been retired to honor past players. For a number to be retired by the Red Sox, the player who used to wear that number must have played for the team for at least ten years and must have been elected to the Baseball Hall of Fame. The numbers that have been retired by The Red Sox are:

> #1 Bobby Doerr
>
> #4 Joe Cronin
>
> #8 Carl Yastrzemski
>
> #9 Ted Williams
>
> #27 Carlton Fisk

Major League Baseball has also retired #42 throughout all of baseball to honor Jackie Robinson who became the first African American to play Major League Baseball back in 1947.

RIGHT FIELD *(noun)*

The portion of the outfield that falls between Centerfield and the Right Field line. Right Field is 380 feet from home plate at its deepest part and is 302 feet along the right field line.

RIGHT FIELD ROOF *(noun)*

Next to Pesky's Pole, above Right Field, and high above the Grand Stand seats is the new Right Field Roof. The beginning of the 2004 season marked the opening of this new section where fans can sit at tables overlooking the outfield and take in the ball game in a whole new way.

ROLLING RALLY PARADE (noun)

The World Series Victory Parade. If there was ever a reason to have a parade it was after an 86 year World Series drought came to an end in 2004. The team boarded Boston Duck Boats, departed Fenway Park, and rode through the streets of Boston and into the Charles River while being cheered by millions of fans. In 2007 a rolling rally parade rolled through the streets again. Although the duck boats didn't splash into the river, fans were nonetheless treated to a *River Dance*. Jonathon Papelbon's celebratory dance entertained fans during the play-offs and, with the help of the Dropkick Murphys, along the parade route.

ROOKIE *(noun)*

A first year player in MLB. Red Sox Second Baseman, Dustin Pedroia, was named Rookie-of-the-Year after the 2007 season. His batting average was .299, he hit 10 homeruns, and had 57 runs batted in.

ROUNDING THE BASES *(verb)*

As a player runs from first base, to second base, to third base, and on towards home plate he is rounding the bases.

RUBBER GAME *(noun)*

A tie breaking game during a series between teams. When two teams have each won one game during a three game series, the third game would be called the rubber game.

RUN *(noun)*

When a player makes it to home plate safely. Runs are scored and recorded and it is the team with the most runs that wins the game.

RUNS BATTED IN (RBI) *(noun)*

The number of runs a batter is responsible for getting across home plate. When runners are on base and a batter hits the ball and gets them to home plate safely the batter is credited with a RBI. If a player hits a homerun he is also credited with a RBI for getting himself to home plate and scoring a run.

SACRIFICE FLY (noun)

When a fly ball is hit deep into the outfield giving another runner the chance to make it to the next base, but results in the current batter getting out.

SAFE (adjective)

When any runner advances to any base without being tagged out. It is up to the umpire to decide if the runner is safe or out.

SAVE (noun)

A credit given to a relief pitcher that ends a game when the opposing team has the opportunity to tie the score or win but then does not.

SCORE (verb)

To get across home plate and earn a run.

(noun)

The number of runs that each team has.

SCOREBOARD (noun)

The place on the left field wall or "Green Monster" that tells fans who the visiting team is, what inning the game is in, how many runs, hits, and errors have occurred, what the ball/strike count is, and what the scores of games being played elsewhere are.

The scoreboard at Fenway Park is famous because it is one of the last manual or hand-operated scoreboards in Major League Baseball.

SCORING POSITION *(noun)*

Being on 2nd or 3rd base and ready to be driven in to score by the batter at the plate.

SECOND BASE *(noun)*

The base that sits 90 feet past first base and 90 feet before third base. The distance between second base and home plate is 127 feet 3 3/8 inches.

SECOND BASEMAN *(noun)*

The infielder responsible for covering second base. It isn't uncommon to see second basemen leaping high into the air to jump over an incoming runner while trying to complete a double play with a throw to first.

SEVENTH INNING STRETCH *(noun)*

The time in between the top and bottom of the seventh inning when the fans stand up and stretch their legs and sing *Take Me Out to the Ballgame* (on Sundays and holidays *God Bless America* is played).

It is said that President Taft should be credited with the very first 7th inning stretch because he once stood up during a game to stretch and the crowd stood up with him to show their respect.

SHORT STOP *(noun)*

The player who plays the fielding position between second and third base. There is a player between 2nd and 3rd base, but not between 1st and 2nd because more batters are right-handed and tend to hit the ball there more often.

SIGNS *(noun)*

The hand motions that the catcher makes to the pitcher to indicate what type of pitch to throw. Coaches will also communicate with players by using predetermined hand signals or signs and the runners on base will too.

SINGLE *(noun)*

When a batter gets a hit and is able to run to first base safely.

SLIDE *(verb)*

When a runner decides to get low to the ground and slide to the base feet or head first to escape being tagged out.

SOUVENIR *(noun)*

Anything that a fan can buy to help remember a day at the park. Souvenirs such as shirts, hats, banners, stuffed Wally dolls, foam #1s, baseballs, miniature bats, flags, and photographs can be bought.

SPRING TRAINING *(noun)*

A baseball team's pre-season program of exercise, practice, and exhibition games from early March to mid-April. The Red Sox team has conducted spring training at City of Palms Park in Fort Myers, Florida since 1993.

STAFF *(noun)*

Employees at the ballpark who are always ready and willing to help fans in any way possible.

STARTING PITCHER *(noun)*

A pitcher who begins the game. Typically a team has five starting pitchers who will rotate starts. It is accepted that it takes at least four days of rest for a starting pitcher to be able to pitch well again.

STEAL *(verb)*

When a runner is able to advance to the next base during a pitch.

STRANDED *(adjective)*

Being on base but not getting home to score before the inning ends.

STRIKE *(noun)*

When a batter swings and misses the ball or when a pitch is thrown within the strike zone without the batter swinging. If a batter has three strikes called he is out.

STRIKE ZONE *(noun)*

The area between a batter's knees and armpits and over home plate. The umpire is responsible for determining if a pitch is thrown within a batter's strike zone.

SUBSTITUTION *(noun)*

When one player comes into the game to take the place of another. The player who leaves the game may not return.

SUPERSTITION *(noun)*

Something that a player feels like he has to do in order to play well. Many professional athletes are superstitious and feel they have to do, wear, or eat certain things before or during a game.

SUSPENDED GAME *(noun)*

A game that is stopped and will be finished on a different day.

SWITCH HITTER *(noun)*

A player who is able to bat left or right-handed.

SWEEP *(verb)*

When one team wins all of the games in a particular series. The Red Sox must have a pretty big broom closet because they swept the St. Louis Cardinals during the 2004 World Series and swept the Colorado Rockies during the 2007 World Series.

SWEET CAROLINE *(proper noun)*

A song sung by Neil Diamond. *Sweet Caroline* is played during the eighth inning and has become a fan favorite at Fenway Park. There is nothing quite like hearing thousands of fans joining together in a sing-along to rally the team!

TAG *(verb)*

To either touch a runner with the ball (or the hand that is holding the ball) or to touch the base while holding the ball before the runner gets there.

TEDDY EBERSON'S RED SOX FIELDS *(noun)*

A series of three baseball/softball diamonds, t-ball diamond, five youth soccer fields, and one regulation-sized soccer field along the Charles River that were made possible by a partnership between the Red Sox, Hill House, and the Esplanade Association. The facility is named in memory of a young Red Sox fan who passed away shortly after his favorite team won the 2004 World Series.

TED WILLIAMS *(proper noun)*

A member of The Red Sox between 1939–1942 and again from 1946–1960. Ted Williams was undoubtedly one of the best Left Fielders to ever play the game. He was also the last player to hit over .400 and his 1941 AVG of .406 later gave Fenway's .406 Club its name. He was inducted into the Baseball Hall of Fame and his famous #9 has been retired by the Red Sox. In 2002 Fenway Park hosted a tribute ceremony to honor Ted Williams after he passed away. A striking bronzed statue was unveiled outside of Fenway's Gate B. Seat number 21 in Section 42 Row 37 in the Right Field Bleachers is painted red to commemorate where the longest measurable homerun ever hit inside Fenway Park landed on June 9th, 1946. That homerun was hit over 502 feet by Ted Williams!

TESSIE *(proper noun)*

A song originally sung by a group of fans called *The Royal Rooter* during the 1903 World Series. In 2004, The Dropkick Murphys recorded an updated version that caught on with fans that year. In the 2007 season, the popular song was *Shipping Up To Boston,* which pitcher Jonathan Papelbon danced to after post-season victories

THIRD BASE (noun)

The last base on the path to Home Plate. Also known as the *hot corner*, third base sits just 90 feet away from home, but can feel like 2 miles for a runner waiting to be batted in. Third Base is 127 feet 3 3/8 inches away from First Base so a player must be able to throw well and accurately to make an out at first.

THIRD BASEMAN (noun)

One of the infielders. The Third Baseman is responsible for covering his base and fielding balls that come near him in the infield.

TRADE (verb)

When a team's management decides to switch one of its current players for one or possibly more players from another team or teams. Managers from both teams and the players' agents become involved in the trade negotiations. July 31st is the trade deadline for teams to make any trade activity.

(noun)

The deal that is made.

TRIPLE (noun)

When a batter is able to run all the way to third base due to one hit.

TRIPLE PLAY (noun)

When three outs are made during one play.

TROPHY (noun)

The prize given to the World Series Champions. The trophy is actually called the Commissioner's Trophy and it was first presented in 1967. The trophy weighs 30 pounds, is 2 feet high, and measures 36 inches around the bottom. The trophy is made of sterling silver and is decorated with 30 flags to represent each team in Major League Baseball.

UMPIRE *(noun)*

The person responsible for calling all pitches and deciding the outcome of all plays during the course of the game. The umpire may remove any player, coach, or person from the game if he should see fit.

UNEARNED RUN *(noun)*

A run that is scored due to an error made by the other team. This run is not included in any batter's RBI as he is not responsible for scoring the run.

USHER *(noun)*

The staff members who help you find your seat within the ballpark.

UTILITY PLAYER *(noun)*

A player who is able to play many different positions.

VISITING TEAM *(noun)*

The team who is not playing at their home field. Every team is the visiting team for half of their games during the season. The visiting team always bats first.

VICTORY *(noun)*

A win. Victories at Fenway Park are always celebrated wildly and the song *Dirty Water* by The Standells plays over the speaker system as soon as the game ends.

WALLY THE GREEN MONSTER

(proper noun)

Wally is the official mascot of the Red Sox. He was first introduced in 1997 and is named after the left field wall which is also named "The Green Monster."

WALK *(verb)*

When a pitcher throws four balls to a batter that batter is then allowed to walk to first base. When the bases are loaded a runner can actually get walked in to score a run.

WALK-OFF HOMER *(noun)*

A homerun that is hit during the bottom of the ninth inning to break a tie and also end the game. Once that team scores a run they can stop batting because it is impossible for the other team to tie the game since they have no more turns to bat. It is called a Walk-off Homer because the players can actually walk off the field because the game is over.

WARM UPS *(noun)*

Many players take time right before the game begins to warm up on the field. It is important that the players stretch and get loose before going out to play.

WAVE (noun)

Fans sitting in the bleachers will start to cheer by rising up with their arms pointed skyward and then sitting down. As fans in each section repeat this motion around the ballpark it creates the effect of an ocean wave rolling through the seats. Usually the wave rolls around the park a couple of times and then fans start paying more attention to the game and the wave peters out.

WILD CARD (noun)

Both the National League and the American League are made up of three divisions called the East, West, and Central. At the end of the season the first place team from the three divisions in each league earns a berth in the play-offs. Eight teams are needed to fill out the play-off roster so the remaining teams in each league compete for the last two seats in the play-offs. The teams with the best records in their respective league are awarded the Wild Card berth. Winning the Wild Card means joining the six first place teams in the play-offs.

WILD PITCH (noun)

A pitch that is thrown far outside of the batter's strike zone and beyond the catcher's reach.

WIN-LOSS PERCENTAGE (noun)

A statistic that represents how many of the games pitched have resulted in wins as opposed to losses.

To figure out the win-loss percentage you take

$$wins \div (wins + losses)$$

So if a pitcher has been awarded 13 wins and 10 losses it would look like this:

$13 \div (13 + 10)$ or $13 \div 23$ which equals .570

WORLD CHAMPIONS (noun)

The World Series winners. To win the World Series a team must win four of the seven games in the series between the American League and National League Champions.

WORLD SERIES (proper noun)

The winner of the American League Championship Series and the National League Championship Series play each other in the World Series. The first World Series was played in 1903.

eXtra innings *(noun)*

Any game that goes past the regulation nine innings of play to break a tie. The longest game ever was on May 9, 1984 between the Chicago Cubs and the Milwaukee Brewers. That game lasted 25 innings and took eight hours and six minutes to play.

Yawkey Way *(proper noun)*

One of the streets that borders Fenway Park. Yawkey Way stretches from Gate A to Gate D and is now only accessible to ticketed fans during game hours. Yawkey Way is named after Tom Yawkey, the former owner of the Boston Red Sox. Yawkey Way is a part of the entire Fenway experience.

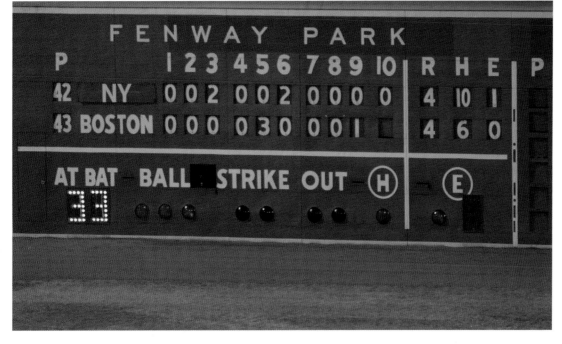

Zero *(noun)*

The number of hits given up by a pitcher in a No-Hitter. Red Sox pitcher, Clay Buchholz, threw a No-Hitter in September 2007, five years after the Red Sox previous No-Hitter. He became the first Red Sox rookie and 17th Red Sox player to ever pitch a no hitter.

GAME STATISTICS

Date _____ Game No. _____ Red Sox vs. _____

Seat: Section _____ Row _____ No. _____

Starting Line-Ups

	Red Sox	_____
Pitcher	_____	_____
Catcher	_____	_____
1st Base	_____	_____
2nd Base	_____	_____
3rd Base	_____	_____
Short Stop	_____	_____
Right Field	_____	_____
Center Field	_____	_____
Left Field	_____	_____
Designated Hitter	_____	_____

Scoreboard Activity

	1st	2nd	3rd	4th	5th	6th	7th	8th	9th	10th	11th
Visitor											
Boston											

	Total	Hits	Runs	Errors
Visitor				
Boston				

Final Score: Red Sox _____ Visitors _____

Who hit Home Runs?

Red Sox	Visitors
_____	_____
_____	_____
_____	_____
_____	_____

Who hit Grand Slams?

Red Sox	Visitors
_____	_____
_____	_____

Were there any records set today?

_____

Who threw out the Ceremonial First Pitch?

_____

Who sang the National Anthem?

_____

Who was the "Down on the Farm Player of the Game"?

_____

Who was the "Red Sox Hero of the Day"?

_____

Who was today's MVP?

_____

AMERICAN LEAGUE

EAST

	Date	Score
❏ Boston Red Sox		
❏ New York Yankees		
❏ Baltimore Orioles		
❏ Tampa Bay Devil Rays		
❏ Toronto Blue Jays		

CENTRAL

	Date	Score
❏ Minnesota Twins		
❏ Chicago White Sox		
❏ Cleveland Indians		
❏ Detroit Tigers		
❏ Kansas City Royals		

WEST

	Date	Score
❏ Anaheim Angels		
❏ Oakland Athletics		
❏ Texas Rangers		
❏ Seattle Mariners		

NATIONAL LEAGUE

EAST

	Date	Score
❏ Atlanta Braves		
❏ Philadelphia Phillies		
❏ Florida Marlins		
❏ New York Mets		
❏ Washington Nationals		

CENTRAL

	Date	Score
❏ St. Louis Cardinals		
❏ Houston Astros		
❏ Chicago Cubs		
❏ Cincinnati Reds		
❏ Pittsburgh Pirates		
❏ Milwaukee Brewers		

WEST

	Date	Score
❏ Los Angeles Dodgers		
❏ San Francisco Giants		
❏ San Diego Padres		
❏ Colorado Rockies		
❏ Arizona Diamond Backs		

AUTOGRAPHS